PHILADELPHIA EAGLES

by Tom Robinson

Published by ABDO Publishing Company, 8000 West 78th Street, Edina, Minnesota 55439. Copyright © 2011 by Abdo Consulting Group, Inc. International copyrights reserved in all countries. No part of this book may be reproduced in any form without written permission from the publisher. SportsZone™ is a trademark and logo of ABDO Publishing Company.

Printed in the United States of America,
North Mankato, Minnesota
062010
092010

Editor: Matt Tustison
Copy Editor: Nicholas Cafarelli
Interior Design and Production: Craig Hinton
Cover Design: Craig Hinton

Photo Credits: Erich Schlegel/AP Images, cover; NFL Photos/AP Images, title page, 4, 7, 8, 13, 20, 33, 42 (bottom), 43 (middle), AP Images, 10, 14, 17, 18, 29, 42 (top and middle); Paul Vathis/AP Images, 22; Rusty Kennedy/AP Images, 24; G. Paul Burnett, File/AP Images, 27, 43 (top); Amy Sancetta/AP Images, 30; David Stluka/AP Images, 35; Mark Lennihan/APImages, 36; Evan Vucci/AP Images, 39; Gene J. Puskar/AP Images, 41, 43 (bottom); Kevin Terrell/AP Images, 44; Paul Spinelli/AP Images, 47

Library of Congress Cataloging-in-Publication Data
Robinson, Tom, 1972-
  Philadelphia Eagles / Tom Robinson.
    p. cm. — (Inside the NFL)
  Includes index.
  ISBN 978-1-61714-024-2
  1. Philadelphia Eagles (Football team)—History—Juvenile literature. I. Title.
  GV956.P44R63 2011
  796.332'640974811—dc22
                        2010017457

TABLE OF CONTENTS

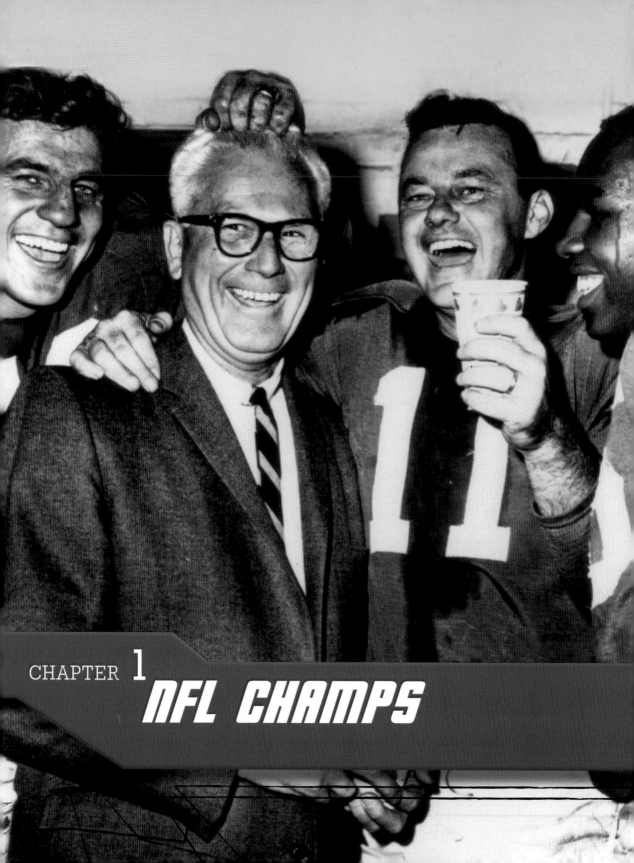

CHAPTER 1
NFL CHAMPS

Chuck Bednarik had the reputation of being one of the toughest players in the National Football League (NFL). He played for the Philadelphia Eagles from the late 1940s to the early 1960s.

New York Giants running back Frank Gifford found out just how tough Bednarik was on November 20, 1960. The host Giants were trying to rally for a win that would allow them to pass the Eagles into first place.

Gifford caught a fourth-quarter pass as he moved across the middle of the field. He kept running toward the out-of-bounds

CHUCK BEDNARIK

Chuck Bednarik became an All-America center at the University of Pennsylvania. This occurred after he had earned an Air Medal for his service in the Army Air Corps during World War II. Bednarik was the first player selected in the 1949 NFL Draft. He took over for the Eagles as starting center and linebacker. Bednarik was a punishing hitter at 233 pounds. He became an NFL Pro Bowl linebacker for five straight seasons, from 1950 to 1954. A native of Bethlehem, Pennsylvania, Bednarik made the Pro Bowl eight times in his 14-year career. He missed only three games.

LEFT TO RIGHT, EAGLES LINEBACKER/CENTER CHUCK BEDNARIK, COACH BUCK SHAW, QUARTERBACK NORM VAN BROCKLIN, AND RUNNING BACK TED DEAN CELEBRATE WINNING THE 1960 NFL TITLE.

CHAMPIONSHIP SEASON

Philadelphia lost the 1960 season opener 41–24 to the Cleveland Browns. The Eagles then won nine straight games. That streak included a 31–29 victory over the Browns in a rematch.

Philadelphia won the Eastern Conference with a 10–2 record. Cleveland went 8–3–1 for the second-best record in the East and the NFL. The Eagles ranked sixth in the league in total offense and seventh in total defense.

Don Burroughs intercepted nine passes. Norm Van Brocklin earned Most Valuable Player honors in his final year before retiring. He took advantage of the big-play abilities of Pete Retzlaff and Tommy McDonald. Retzlaff caught 46 passes for 826 yards. McDonald had 39 catches for 801 yards and 13 touchdowns. Retzlaff, McDonald, and Bobby Walston all ranked in the top 10 in the league in yards per catch.

line and a chance to stop the clock. But Bednarik had a clean shot at him. "Concrete Charlie," as the Eagles' linebacker was sometimes known, delivered a crushing blow. It sent Gifford flying to the ground, flat on his back. He was unconscious.

The hit had a big impact on the 1960 NFL title race. The ball left Gifford's hands before he hit the ground. The Eagles recovered the fumble to clinch a 17–10 win.

Gifford missed the rest of the 1960 season and the 1961 season with a concussion. The Giants ended the day 1.5 games behind the Eagles in the Eastern Conference. With New York missing Gifford for the rematch the next weekend, Philadelphia won again 31–23. This virtually ended the East title race. The Eagles finished the regular season 10–2.

THE EAGLES' CHUCK BEDNARIK WAS THE LAST FULL-TIME TWO-WAY PLAYER IN THE NFL. HE PLAYED LINEBACKER ON DEFENSE AND CENTER ON OFFENSE.

Bednarik played a huge role as the Eagles won the 1960 NFL championship. He was the last of the league's full-time two-way players. In addition to being a linebacker, he was regarded as one of the league's best centers.

Bednarik was on the field for 58 of the 60 minutes when Philadelphia faced the Western Conference champion Green Bay Packers in the NFL Championship Game. It was held on December 26 in Philadelphia.

THE EAGLES' TED DEAN, *RIGHT*, RUNS AGAINST THE PACKERS DURING THE 1960 NFL TITLE GAME. PHILADELPHIA WON 17–13.

The Eagles scored the only touchdown of the first three quarters. Quarterback Norm Van Brocklin had been chosen as the NFL's Most Valuable Player (MVP) that season. He found wide receiver Tommy McDonald for a 35-yard touchdown pass in the second quarter. It erased a 6–0 lead that Green Bay had built on two field goals by kicker Paul Hornung. Philadelphia headed to the fourth quarter ahead 10–6.

Bart Starr hit wide receiver Max McGee with a 7-yard touchdown pass to put the Packers in front 13–10. Philadelphia's

ENDING ON A HIGH NOTE

Norm Van Brocklin was unhappy sharing time at quarterback with the Los Angeles Rams. After the 1957 season, he said he was retiring from football. He had played for the Rams since 1949. The future Hall of Fame player returned when Los Angeles traded his rights to Philadelphia before the 1958 season. The Eagles gave up defensive back Jimmy Harris, guard Buck Lansford, and a first-round draft pick. Van Brocklin played three years in Philadelphia before retiring for good after leading the Eagles to the 1960 NFL championship.

Ted Dean returned the following kickoff 58 yards. The return set up Dean's 5-yard run for the go-ahead touchdown with 5:21 remaining. It proved to be the game-winning score.

Starr led Green Bay back down the field to take a shot at pulling out the win. Bednarik was there to make sure the championship did not get away. Bednarik stopped Packers running back Jim Taylor at the 8-yard line. Then he held Taylor down a couple of seconds longer. The clock ran out before the Packers could try one more play. It had looked as if Taylor had room to run for the score before Bednarik made the stop. However, Bednarik's tackle secured the 17–13 championship game victory.

Today, the Super Bowl champion receives the Vince Lombardi Trophy, named after the legendary Packers coach. Vince Lombardi lost one playoff game in his career—the 1960 NFL Championship Game against Philadelphia. His Packers teams went 9–1 in playoff games and won five league titles.

"That game, without a doubt, was the greatest game I ever had," Bednarik said years later.

CHAPTER 2

THE EARLY YEARS

The Frankford Yellow Jackets were a professional football team in the suburbs of Philadelphia. They played from 1924 to 1931. The Yellow Jackets sat out the 1932 season of the NFL. The league ran a much less formal schedule in its early days.

Bert Bell and Lud Wray led an investment group that purchased the inactive team for $2,500. They moved it to Philadelphia and renamed it the Philadelphia Eagles in 1933. The Eagles name came from the eagle that was the symbol of the New Deal's National Recovery Act.

After three seasons in which the team lost $80,000, the club folded. The joint ownership group was broken up. The Eagles were offered up at a public auction. This time, Bell bought the team for himself for $4,000.

Bell had served as the Eagles' general manager before

BERT BELL, COACH AND OWNER OF THE EAGLES, TALKS TO HIS SQUAD ON JULY 26, 1939.

he became sole owner. While he was the general manager, he had proposed an annual college draft for the NFL. He believed that a draft would spread the talent around the league more evenly. He feared that certain teams were in position to dominate otherwise. The other owners agreed to the proposed draft and put it into use in 1936.

As owner, Bell added to his responsibilities. He replaced Wray as head coach for the 1936 season. The Eagles won just one game in three of his first five seasons. In fact, the team did not have a winning record in any season in its first decade.

The Eagles finished 1–9–1 in 1939. But they found other ways to generate some excitement. The team signed Davey O'Brien, an All-America quarterback from Texas Christian University, to a large contract. He set an NFL record with 1,324 passing yards in his rookie season.

Pro football in Pennsylvania underwent some changes in 1940. That is when Pittsburgh Steelers owner Art Rooney sold his stake in the team to Alexis Thompson. Rooney then bought half interest in the Eagles. But one year later, Rooney returned to Pittsburgh. Rooney took Bell with him and swapped franchises with Thompson.

EARLE "GREASY" NEALE WAS COACH OF THE EAGLES FROM 1941 TO 1950, INCLUDING THE 1943 SEASON OF THE "STEAGLES."

The two teams would soon work together. World War II meant there were fewer available players. So for the 1943 season, the two teams merged and played under the name of "Phil-Pitt Steagles."

SHARING RESOURCES

The Philadelphia Eagles and Pittsburgh Steelers shared everything in the 1943 season under the name of the Phil-Pitt Steagles. Earle "Greasy" Neale of the Eagles and Walt Kiesling of the Steelers served as co-coaches. The roster was split among available players from the two teams. The combined team produced a 5–4–1 record. The winning record was something the Eagles had not accomplished in their first 10 years on their own.

CHAPTER 3

PERFECT DEFENSE

The Phil-Pitt Steagles split up after the 1943 season. Earle "Greasy" Neale was back coaching the Philadelphia Eagles. Under Neale's leadership, the Eagles became a winning team for the first time on their own.

First-round draft pick Steve Van Buren took over at halfback in 1944. The Eagles went 7–1–2 to finish in second place in the Eastern Conference behind the New York Giants (8–1–1).

Philadelphia contended for the title in the years ahead. Future Hall of Famers Van Buren, center/linebacker Alex Wojciechowicz, and end Pete Pihos led the way. The Eagles held second place for three straight seasons.

Van Buren led the NFL in rushing yards and touchdowns four times in five years, beginning with his second season in 1945.

THE EAGLES' FRANK REAGAN INTERCEPTS A PASS INTENDED FOR THE RAMS' BOB SHAW IN THE 1949 NFL CHAMPIONSHIP GAME. PHILADELPHIA WON 14–0.

STEVE VAN BUREN

Steve Van Buren was the leading offensive player on back-to-back Eagles championship teams in 1948 and 1949. He scored the winning touchdown in 1948.

Orphaned as a young boy in Honduras, he became one of the game's great underdog stories. Van Buren moved to New Orleans to live with his grandparents and was unable to make his high school football team as a 125-pound sophomore. In his senior year, Van Buren landed a scholarship to play football at Louisiana State University.

Van Buren played halfback but with the toughness of a fullback. He was a five-time NFL All-Pro. In his second season in 1945, he led the NFL in rushing, scoring, and kick returning.

Van Buren played eight seasons in the NFL, all with Philadelphia. He helped turn the Eagles from a struggling team into a winner. He was enshrined in the Pro Football Hall of Fame in 1965.

He helped make the Eagles the highest-scoring team in the NFL that season. It was defense that eventually put the team on top, however.

The Eagles and Steelers were connected again in 1947. The two Pennsylvania teams tied for first place in the Eastern Conference at 8–4.

This set up a playoff to determine who would face the Chicago Cardinals in the NFL Championship Game. The Eagles allowed the Steelers only seven first downs in a 21–0 shutout victory. Tommy Thompson threw two touchdown passes.

The Cardinals spoiled the Eagles' first championship game appearance. Chicago won 28–21 at home in Comiskey Park. Chicago went ahead by two touchdowns three times.

PETE PIHOS WAS AN EAGLE FROM 1947 TO 1955. HE WAS A KEY MEMBER OF THE 1948 AND 1949 NFL TITLE TEAMS.

Each time Philadelphia came back to get within seven points. The Eagles, however, were never able to put two scores together to erase the deficit.

Philadelphia opened the 1948 season with a tough 21–14 loss to the Cardinals. The Eagles then tied the Los Angeles Rams 28–28 to start the season 0–1–1.

But the team quickly showed that it still had the ability to contend for a title. The Eagles pounded the New York Giants and the Washington Redskins by 45–0 scores in each of the next

STEVE VAN BUREN PLUNGES OVER THE GOAL LINE FOR THE WINNING TOUCHDOWN IN THE EAGLES' 1948 NFL TITLE GAME WIN OVER THE CARDINALS.

two weeks. Philadelphia finished with four shutouts on the way to a 9–2–1 record.

The Cardinals and Eagles played again on December 19 in the NFL Championship Game. There was a heavy snowstorm at Shibe Park in Philadelphia.

The conditions limited the teams to five combined pass completions with three interceptions. The Eagles recovered a fumble at the

Cardinals' 17-yard line in the fourth quarter and took advantage. Van Buren ran 5 yards for the game's only score. The Eagles earned their first NFL title with a 7–0 win.

Linebacker/center Chuck Bednarik joined when the Eagles picked him first in the 1949 NFL Draft. Bednarik had earned All-America honors at the University of Pennsylvania. He became part of an Eagles team that won its third straight NFL Eastern Conference title in 1949.

The 1949 team, arguably the greatest in Eagles history, went 11–1. They led the league in scoring with 364 points and gave up a league-low 134. Philadelphia finished the regular season with eight straight wins by two touchdowns or more.

Including the championship game, the Eagles did not allow a touchdown in their three games in December.

Van Buren ran for a team playoff-record 196 yards, and the Eagles became the first team in NFL history to win two straight championship games by shutout when they stopped the Los Angeles Rams 14–0. The Rams averaged less than 1 yard per running play. The Eagles allowed only seven first downs.

FOR STARTERS

The Eagles never fared better than 7–4 –1 in a season in the 1950s. They were not able to return to the playoffs between their 1949 and 1960 championship seasons. The Eagles struggled in the late 1950s and early 1960s as two players who became NFL offensive stars were getting their careers started with them. Quarterback Sonny Jurgensen played for Philadelphia from 1957 to 1963. He would become a standout with the Washington Redskins through 1974. Wide receiver Tommy McDonald also was with the Eagles from 1957 to 1963. He then played five more seasons with four other teams. Both players went on to become Hall of Famers.

CHAPTER 4

THE LONG WAIT

The defending NFL champion Eagles were tied with the New York Giants for first place in the Eastern Conference. The teams met December 10 at Franklin Field in Philadelphia in the next-to-last game of the 1961 season.

Eagles quarterback Sonny Jurgensen was on his way to producing the best single-season passing numbers in team history. Jurgensen had replaced Norm Van Brocklin, who retired after the 1960 title season.

Jurgensen teamed up with Tommy McDonald to try to bring the Eagles back after the Giants took a 21–10 lead. Jurgensen threw for 367 yards and three

BOB "THE BOOMER" BROWN

Bob "The Boomer" Brown was named college football's Lineman of the Year in 1963 while playing guard at the University of Nebraska. He was then picked in the first round of the 1964 NFL Draft by Philadelphia. Brown made the Pro Bowl three times in his five seasons with the Eagles. He then played for the Los Angeles Rams and Oakland Raiders through 1973. Although bothered by a knee injury, Brown completed a career that landed him in the Pro Football Hall of Fame.

CHUCK BEDNARIK WALKS OFF THE FIELD DURING THE EAGLES' 19–14 LOSS TO THE GIANTS IN NOVEMBER 1962.

OFFENSIVE TACKLE BOB "THE BOOMER" BROWN PLAYED FOR THE EAGLES FROM 1964 TO 1968 AND WAS ONE OF THEIR KEY PLAYERS.

touchdowns. He twice brought the Eagles back to within four points. McDonald had seven catches for 237 yards and two scores. But Philadelphia lost 28–24.

The Eagles won their next game, and the Giants tied their season finale. That left the Eagles at 10–4. They were a half-game short of repeating as division champions and getting a chance to defend their title in the NFL Championship Game.

The near miss turned out to be the start of a 17-year playoff drought. The 1966 team went 9–5 for the only winning record in that stretch. The trouble started when the 1962 team was wiped out by a series of injuries and went from 10–4 the year before to 3–10–1. In just two years, the Eagles had dropped from league champion to last place in the division.

In the 1970s, the Eagles started adding the pieces that would allow the team to be successful again. Wide receiver Harold Carmichael, the team's all-time receiving leader, was drafted in 1971. All-Pro linebacker Bill Bergey came to the team in a trade with the Cincinnati Bengals in 1974. Dick Vermeil left the University of California, Los Angeles (UCLA) to become head coach of the Eagles in 1976. A trade with the Los Angeles Rams brought quarterback Ron Jaworski to Philadelphia in 1977. It was the last year of the 17 without a playoff appearance.

INVINCIBLE

Vince Papale, a school teacher and coach from Philadelphia, never played college football. However, he did make it in the NFL.

With the team struggling, Eagles coach Dick Vermeil held tryouts. Papale, who played for a semiprofessional squad in the area, attended and made his way onto the roster in 1976 as a special teams player. Papale became a fan favorite. He wound up being the Eagles' special teams captain.

"Coach Vermeil always told me that when I made a tackle on special teams, the Veterans Stadium turf would shake," Papale said. "...He gave me an opportunity and a chance that nobody else in the NFL would have."

Papale's story was told in the 2006 movie *Invincible*. Mark Wahlberg played Papale in the movie. Papale received the Vince Lombardi Award for Courage after overcoming colon cancer. He now serves as a motivational speaker.

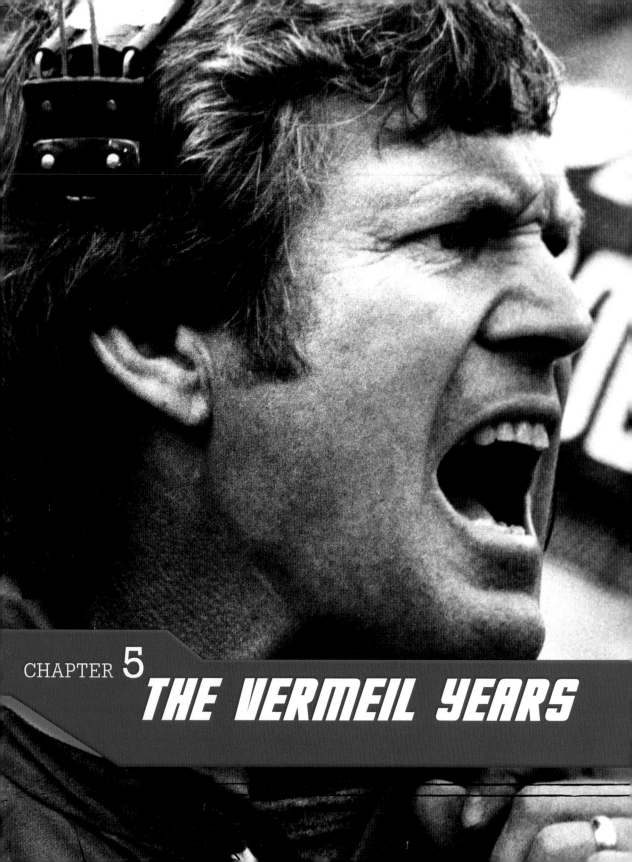

CHAPTER 5
THE VERMEIL YEARS

The Eagles were improving in 1978, Dick Vermeil's third season as coach. The team had a 6–5 record when it went to the Meadowlands to play the New York Giants on November 19. The Giants had a 17–12 lead in the final minute. The Eagles were out of timeouts.

All the Giants needed to do was have quarterback Joe Pisarcik take the snap and kneel to down the ball. Then the clock would run out.

The Giants took a different approach—and paid the price.

Pisarcik turned to hand off to fullback Larry Csonka. But as Pisarcik reached to put the ball in Csonka's arms, the ball instead hit Csonka's hip and bounced free. Pisarcik reached to retrieve the ball. It bounced again, this time into the hands

DICK VERMEIL LED THE EAGLES TO FOUR PLAYOFF APPEARANCES AND A SUPER BOWL IN HIS TIME AS THEIR COACH, FROM 1976 TO 1982.

TIMELY HIT

Bill Bergey credited fellow Eagles linebacker Frank LeMaster with setting up the "Miracle at the Meadowlands." The fumble return in the final minute allowed Philadelphia to edge the New York Giants 19–17 in 1978 and sent the team on its way to a playoff berth.

In 2009, Bergey told Comcast Sports that LeMaster fired through the line and hit Giants quarterback Joe Pisarcik as he took a knee on the previous play. The teams started fighting and had to be separated. On the next play, Pisarcik tried to hand off instead of kneeling again to end the game. When he did, Pisarcik and fullback Larry Csonka fumbled the exchange. This allowed Herman Edwards to come up with the ball and run it in for the winning touchdown.

Edwards later became an NFL coach. He served as coach of the New York Jets from 2001 to 2005 and the Kansas City Chiefs from 2006 to 2008.

of Eagles cornerback Herman Edwards.

Edwards took off on an improbable 26-yard touchdown return with 20 seconds left. "It seemed like everything about that play happened in slow motion," Edwards said. "The ball fell right in front of me and took a perfect hop."

The play, which became known as the "Miracle at the Meadowlands," turned around the Eagles' fortunes. The game meant the difference between an 8–8 finish and a 9–7 season. It was Philadelphia's first winning record in a dozen years and its first playoff appearance since 1960.

"That one game started the snowball rolling," Eagles linebacker Bill Bergey said. "For years, the Eagles were a team that couldn't catch a break.

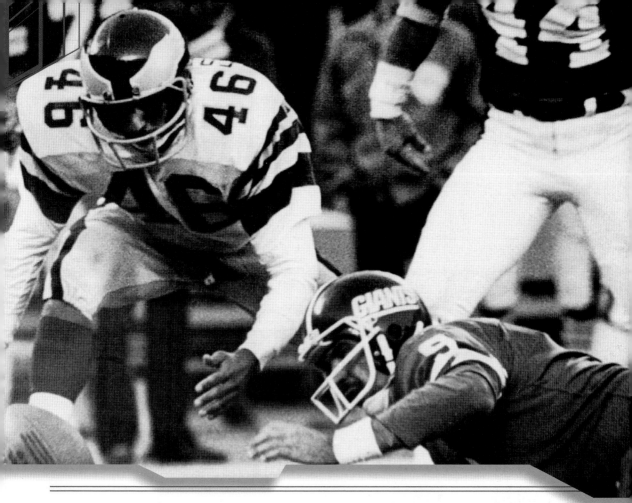

EAGLES CORNERBACK HERMAN EDWARDS PICKS UP A FUMBLE BY GIANTS QUARTERBACK JOE PISARCIK IN THE "MIRACLE AT THE MEADOWLANDS" GAME IN 1978.

Suddenly, we were winning with a doggone miracle. It was like, 'Now it's our turn.' We came of age as a team that day."

When NFL Films made its "The 100 Greatest Touchdowns" video in 1993, the play was ranked at number 10 out of the more than 40,000 touchdowns that had been scored in the league's history.

The 1978 season started a stretch of four straight in which the Eagles made the playoffs.

The 1980 team was the most accomplished of those playoff squads. It set a club record with 12 wins. Then the team defeated the East Division rival Dallas Cowboys 20–7 in the National Football Conference (NFC) Championship Game in Philadelphia.

A NEW STREAK

After 17 straight years out of the playoffs, the Eagles made it to the postseason four straight times from 1978 to 1981. The return to the playoffs resulted in a 14–13 loss in 1978. The Atlanta Falcons scored two fourth-quarter touchdowns to beat the Eagles. The 1979 team won its wild-card round game, 27–17 over the Chicago Bears. But then the Eagles were upset 24–17 by the Tampa Bay Buccaneers in the divisional round. The 1980 team went to the Super Bowl with wins over the Minnesota Vikings (31–16) and Dallas Cowboys (20–7) in the NFC playoffs. Wilbert Montgomery rushed for 194 yards against the Cowboys to send the Eagles to the Super Bowl. The Oakland Raiders won the Super Bowl 27–10, however. The last playoff game in the Eagles' four-year streak was a 27–21 loss to the New York Giants after the 1981 season.

The Eagles advanced to Super Bowl XV against the Oakland Raiders. The game was held on January 25, 1981, in New Orleans, Louisiana. The Raiders became the first wild-card team to win a Super Bowl.

Raiders Linebacker Rod Martin intercepted three passes by Ron Jaworski. Oakland quarterback Jim Plunkett threw for three touchdowns in the game. The Raiders beat the Eagles 27–10. Plunkett's 80-yard touchdown pass to Kenny King gave the Raiders a 14–0 lead in the closing seconds of the first quarter.

Philadelphia began to struggle even before its run of playoff appearances ended. The Eagles started the 1981 season 6–0. But they lost six of their remaining 10 games before losing in the wild-card round of the playoffs.

PHILADELPHIA QUARTERBACK RON JAWORSKI TRIES TO SCRAMBLE AWAY FROM OAKLAND DEFENSIVE END JOHN MATUSZAK IN SUPER BOWL XV.

Vermeil resigned at the end of the strike-shortened 1982 season. The 1983 team went from a 4–2 start to seven straight losses and a 5–11 final record. The 1984 and 1985 teams played better later in the season. But neither could overcome a 1–4 start.

ONE-TWO PUNCH

The Eagles' all-time leading rusher and all-time leading receiver played together for seven seasons from 1977 to 1983. Wilbert Montgomery rushed for 6,538 yards for Philadelphia from 1977 to 1984. He finished his career with the Detroit Lions in 1985. Harold Carmichael caught 589 passes for 8,978 yards with the Eagles (1971–83). He played all but two games of his career with the team. He retired after a brief stint with the rival Dallas Cowboys in 1984.

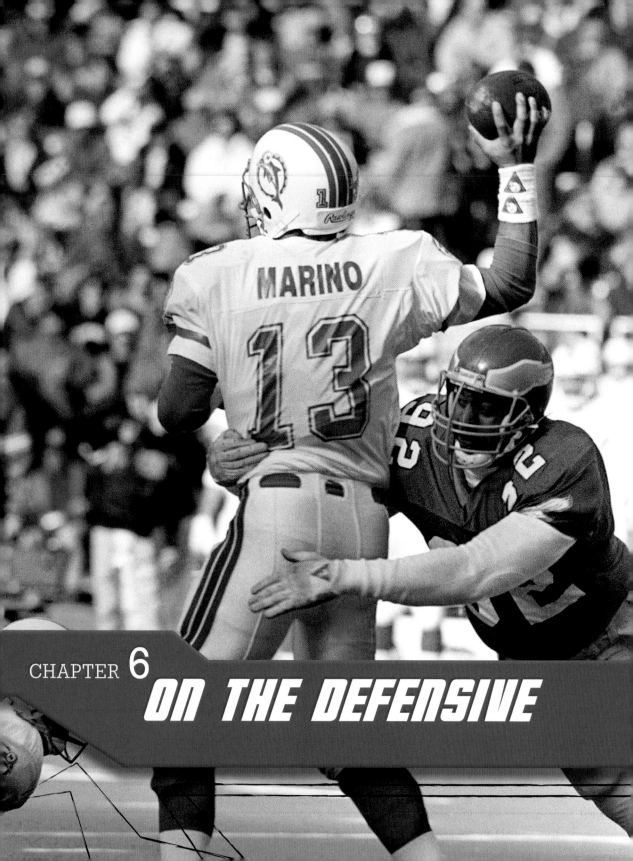

CHAPTER 6
ON THE DEFENSIVE

The offense had its moments. But the Eagles teams that made the playoffs three times under Buddy Ryan and twice under Ray Rhodes in the 1980s and 1990s were known for their defense. That was not surprising since Ryan and Rhodes made names for themselves as defensive coaches before becoming head coaches.

Ryan was the defensive coordinator for the dominant 1985 Chicago Bears championship team. He then led the Eagles to the playoffs from 1988 to 1990. Those were the last three of his five seasons as their coach. Rhodes had been a defensive coordinator with the San Francisco 49ers. He was named NFL Coach of the Year when he took the Eagles to the playoffs in 1995, his first season with them. Rhodes repeated that effort in 1996. However, he could not lead the team to the postseason in 1997 or 1998. He was then fired.

Philadelphia had been out of the playoffs for six straight

THE EAGLES' REGGIE WHITE SACKS DOLPHINS QUARTERBACK DAN MARINO IN 1987. WHITE HAD 21 SACKS THAT SEASON DESPITE PLAYING IN ONLY 12 GAMES.

REGGIE WHITE

Reggie White became an ordained Baptist minister at the age of 17 while growing up in Tennessee. By the time he left the University of Tennessee on his way to a pro football career, White was known as "The Minister of Defense."

White got a late start on his NFL career because he spent his first two pro seasons with the United States Football League. The league went out of business in 1985. White made up for lost time when he made his debut with the Eagles in the fourth week of the 1985 season. He was named NFL Defensive Rookie of the Year.

White went on to earn Defensive Player of the Year honors for the Eagles in 1987 and 1991 and the Green Bay Packers in 1998. He retired as the NFL career sacks leader with 198.

The Pro Football Hall of Famer died suddenly of a heart attack the day after Christmas in 2004 at the age of 43.

seasons before the 1988 team finished 6–1 to win the NFC East Division with a 10–6 record.

The Eagles won at least 10 games each season from 1988 through 1992. In 1992, they made the playoffs under Rich Kotite. He was the coach from 1991 to 1994.

For all their regular-season success, the Eagles were unable to win a playoff game under Ryan. After falling to the host Chicago Bears 20–12 in the divisional round in 1988, they lost wild-card games at home the next two years. The Los Angeles Rams ended the Eagles' 1989 season with a 21–7 win. The Washington Redskins ended it the next season with a 20–6 playoff victory.

Eagles starting quarterback Randall Cunningham and his backup, Jim McMahon, were

EAGLES COACH BUDDY RYAN WALKS ON THE SIDELINE DURING PHILADELPHIA'S 20–12 "FOG BOWL" PLAYOFF LOSS AT CHICAGO ON DECEMBER 31, 1988.

lost due to injuries early in the 1991 season. They needed five quarterbacks just to get through the first half of the season with a 3–5 record. But the defense produced another 10-win season. The Eagles led the NFL in sacks, takeaways, rushing yard-age allowed, passing yardage allowed, and total defense.

TRAGIC ACCIDENT

Jerome Brown was coming off a Pro Bowl season when the Philadelphia defensive tackle was killed in a car accident on June 25, 1992, in his hometown of Brooksville, Florida.

THE FOG BOWL

After the 1988 divisional playoff game started under sunny conditions, a thick fog moved in off Lake Michigan. This severely limited visibility for the Chicago Bears' 20–12 victory over the visiting Eagles. In the press box, announcers could no longer accurately describe the action on the field because they could not see it. On the field, the players could not see more than 10 or 15 yards away. "When that fog rolled in, you might as well close your eyes and close up the shop," Philadelphia quarterback Randall Cunningham said 20 years later. "That was it. We could probably have had the whole team on field and people wouldn't have known. Maybe that's what we should have done." Once the fog was in place, each team could only manage to score one field goal in the second half.

Three-fourths of Philadelphia's defensive line—tackle Jerome Brown and ends Reggie White and Clyde Simmons—played in the Pro Bowl.

The Eagles went 11–5 in 1992 and defeated the New Orleans Saints in the wild-card playoff round. The Eagles scored the game's final 29 points, 26 of them in the fourth quarter, for a 36–20 victory. It was Philadelphia's first playoff win since the 1980 team's NFC Championship Game victory. It was also the Eagles' first road playoff win since the 1949 NFL championship team. Cunningham threw two touchdown passes to Fred Barnett. Eric Allen intercepted two passes, one of which he returned for a touchdown. The eventual Super Bowl champion Dallas Cowboys ended the Eagles' season the next week, however, 34–10.

Philadelphia could not produce a winning record in 1993 or 1994. The Eagles, though, were back in the playoffs the next two seasons under Rhodes. That gave Philadelphia six playoff appearances in nine years. The 1995 team opened a 51–7 lead on the Detroit Lions in the third quarter of a 58–37 playoff

RANDALL CUNNINGHAM, SHOWN IN 1992, PLAYED QUARTERBACK FOR THE EAGLES FROM 1985 TO 1995 AND WAS KNOWN FOR HIS ABILITY TO RUN AS WELL AS PASS.

victory. But the Eagles fell to the Cowboys a week later 30–11.

The Eagles again lost their starting quarterback in 1996, when Rodney Peete hurt his knee. Ty Detmer took over. He led Philadelphia to four straight wins and a playoff berth with a 10–6 record. The 49ers ended the Eagles' season with a 14–0 win in a wild-card playoff game in the rain in San Francisco.

CHAPTER 7

ROUGH START

Philadelphia sports fans have a reputation for being noisy. The fans can be very tough on referees and opponents. As quarterback Donovan McNabb found out the day he was drafted, they can even be tough on their own players, coaches, and teams.

The Eagles held the second overall pick in the 1999 NFL Draft. Some of the team's fans thought that the pick should be used on University of Texas running back Ricky Williams. Knowing that the Eagles planned to pick McNabb, sports talk radio host Angelo Cataldi organized a group of fans to drive to New York City. That is where the draft would be held on April 17.

When NFL commissioner Paul Tagliabue announced that the Eagles had selected McNabb, the team's fans at Madison Square Garden booed loudly.

"All we have to do really is to get everything back to the way it used to be, get back on the winning track, then they'll believe it was the right pick," McNabb said. In an odd way, the

QUARTERBACK DONOVAN MCNABB POSES AFTER PHILADELPHIA DRAFTED HIM IN 1999 IN NEW YORK. MANY EAGLES FANS BOOED THE PICK.

DONAVAN McNABB

Donovan McNabb was a two-sport standout at Syracuse University. He excelled in football at Syracuse and also performed well for the school's powerhouse basketball program.

In the NFL, McNabb ran better than most quarterbacks and quickly became an effective passer on the professional level. Only John Elway, Fran Tarkenton, and Steve Young have matched McNabb's accomplishment of passing for more than 30,000 yards and 200 touchdowns while running for more than 3,000 yards and 20 touchdowns. Through the 2009 season, McNabb held many of the Eagles' all-time passing records. The six-time Pro Bowl selection also had the lowest percentage of interceptions of any quarterback in NFL history.

In April 2010, the Eagles traded McNabb to the Washington Redskins.

fans' reaction helped the former Syracuse University standout. It provided motivation to prove the doubters wrong.

Andy Reid was the first-year coach who had wanted to draft McNabb to run the Eagles' offense. Reid would win more games than any other Eagles coach, and McNabb would set team passing records. They led five straight teams with 11 or more wins to start the 2000s. Philadelphia went 103–56–1 in the decade. However, the Eagles were known just as much for their four NFC Championship Game losses that kept them from reaching the Super Bowl.

The Eagles reached their second Super Bowl in team history after the 2004 season, however. They finished a team-best 13–3 in the regular season.

COACH ANDY REID AND QUARTERBACK DONOVAN MCNABB LED THE EAGLES TO MANY WINS BUT DID NOT GET THE ULTIMATE VICTORY IN A SUPER BOWL.

The Eagles laid the groundwork for their NFC championship before the season started. They signed free-agent defensive end Jevon Kearse and traded for wide receiver Terrell Owens. McNabb had his best season. He became the first NFL quarterback to throw more than 30 touchdowns and fewer than 10 interceptions in the same season.

Philadelphia breezed into the Super Bowl. The Eagles beat the Minnesota Vikings 27–14 and the Atlanta Falcons 27–10 in the NFC playoffs. Those victories gave the Eagles a shot at the defending champion New England Patriots in Super Bowl XXXIX. The game was held on February 6, 2005, in Jacksonville, Florida.

However, New England would repeat as champion. The Patriots forced four turnovers. Deion Branch was chosen as the game's MVP. He caught 11 passes for 133 yards for New England in its 24–21 victory over Philadelphia.

McNabb hit Greg Lewis with a 30-yard touchdown pass with 1:48 left. The Eagles got the ball back at their 4-yard line with 46 seconds remaining. However, McNabb was intercepted on the series' third play.

The interception ended any hopes of a comeback win.

Philadelphia made the playoffs in eight of 10 seasons during that decade. The 2009 team finished 11–5 despite playing most of the season without star running back Brian Westbrook.

The Eagles made a big decision as they entered the new decade. On April 4, 2010, Philadelphia traded star quarterback McNabb to the Washington Redskins.

"While it has been my goal to win a Super Bowl in Philadelphia, we came up short. I enjoyed my 11 years, and know we shared a lot more good times than bad," McNabb said in a statement after the trade.

Philadelphia decided to give backup quarterback Kevin Kolb a shot. The Eagles had drafted him in the second round in 2007

PHILADELPHIA'S DONOVAN MCNABB TRIES TO GET AWAY FROM NEW ENGLAND'S ROOSEVELT COLVIN IN SUPER BOWL XXXIX. THE PATRIOTS WON 24–21.

out of the University of Houston. Kolb would have talented, young receivers to work with in DeSean Jackson and Jeremy Maclin. The question was whether the Eagles could remain perched in their place among the NFL's top teams. Eagles fans are hoping the new core of young players can keep them among the league's elite teams for years to come.

ANDY REID

Andy Reid took over as Philadelphia's coach after the team went 3–13 in 1998. Through 2009, Reid had twice been named NFL Coach of the Year. He led the Eagles to five NFC Championship Games and one Super Bowl. As of 2010, only Tennessee's Jeff Fisher had been with his team longer among NFL head coaches. Reid is a California native. He was an offensive lineman at Brigham Young University in Utah. He became a quarterbacks coach in Green Bay and an offensive coordinator in San Francisco. He then earned the assignment with Philadelphia.

TIMELINE

1933	The dormant Frankford Yellow Jackets of the NFL are awarded to an ownership group headed by Bert Bell and Lud Wray. The team is moved from the suburbs into the city and renamed the Philadelphia Eagles.
1939	The host Brooklyn Dodgers beat the Eagles 23–14 on October 22 in the first televised NFL game.
1943	During World War II, the Philadelphia Eagles and Pittsburgh Steelers combine for one season as the Phil-Pitt Steagles.
1944	The Eagles post their first winning season.
1947	The Eagles win their first playoff game, shutting out Pittsburgh on December 21 to reach the NFL Championship Game. They lose the title game to the Chicago Cardinals on December 28.
1948	On December 19, Philadelphia beats the Chicago Cardinals 7–0 in the NFL Championship Game.
1949	The Eagles follow up an 11–1 regular season by blanking the Los Angeles Rams 14–0 in the NFL Championship Game on December 18.
1960	Philadelphia beats the Green Bay Packers 17–13 on December 26 for the last of its NFL championships as of 2009.

1961	The Eagles fall a half-game short of winning the East Division and getting a shot to defend their title in the NFL Championship Game.
1978	On November 19, Herman Edwards returns a fumble for a touchdown in the final minute as the Eagles use the "Miracle at the Meadowlands" to end a 17-year playoff drought.
1981	Philadelphia loses 27–10 to the Oakland Raiders on January 25 in its first Super Bowl appearance, after the 1980 regular season.
1988	The Eagles lose the Fog Bowl to the Bears on December 31 in Chicago, 20–12, and are knocked out of the playoffs.
1992	On June 25, Philadelphia standout defensive tackle Jerome Brown dies in an automobile accident in Florida.
1999	Eagles fans at Madison Square Garden boo when the team selects quarterback Donovan McNabb second overall in the NFL Draft on April 17.
2005	On February 6, the Eagles fall 24–21 to the New England Patriots in Super Bowl XXXIX after the 2004 season.
2010	On April 4, the Eagles trade Donavan McNabb, who holds many team passing records, to the Washington Redskins for a second-round draft pick in 2010 and a conditional pick in 2011.

QUICK STATS

FRANCHISE HISTORY

Frankford Yellow Jackets (1924–31)
Philadelphia Eagles (1933–42)
Phil-Pitt Steagles (1943)
Philadelphia Eagles (1944–)

SUPER BOWLS
(wins in bold)

1980 (XV), **2004 (XXXIX)**

NFL CHAMPIONSHIP GAMES
(1933–69; wins in bold)

1947, **1948**, **1949**, **1960**

NFC CHAMPIONSHIP GAMES
(since 1970 AFL-NFL merger)

1980, 2001, 2002, 2003, 2004, 2008

DIVISION CHAMPIONSHIPS
(since 1970 AFL-NFL merger)

1980, 1988, 2001, 2002, 2003, 2004,
2006

KEY PLAYERS
(position, seasons with team)

Chuck Bednarik (C/LB, 1949–62)
Bob "Boomer" Brown (G, 1964–68)
Harold Carmichael (WR, 1971–83)
Randall Cunningham (QB, 1985–95)
Sonny Jurgensen (QB, 1957–63)
Tommy McDonald (WR, 1957–63)
Donovan McNabb (QB, 1999–2009)
Wilbert Montgomery (RB, 1977–84)
Pete Pihos (TE/DE, 1947–55)
Steve Van Buren (RB, 1944–51)
Reggie White (DE, 1985–92)

KEY COACHES

Earle "Greasy" Neale (1941–50):
   63–43–5; 3–1 (playoffs)
Andy Reid (1999–):
   108–67–1; 10–8 (playoffs)

HOME FIELDS

Lincoln Financial Field (2003–)
Veterans Stadium (1971–2002)
Franklin Field (1958–70)
Shibe Park (1940–57)
   Known as Connie Mack Stadium
   starting in 1953
Municipal Stadium (1936–39)
Baker Bowl (1933–35)

* All statistics through 2009 season

QUOTES AND ANECDOTES

Hall of Fame coach Marv Levy was impressed by Andy Reid's work with the Eagles. Levy, who coached the Buffalo Bills to four Super Bowls in the 1990s, said, "What Andy Reid has done is remarkable, especially in light of the salary cap and free agency and the inability to maintain continuity. What I like most about him is he's level-headed. It doesn't concern him who gets the credit. He's not concerned with puffery."

The Eagles and the host Brooklyn Dodgers played in the first televised NFL game on October 22, 1939. NBC made the game available to the approximately 1,000 television sets in existence in Brooklyn.

The Eagles selected defensive tackle Jerome Brown ninth in the 1987 NFL Draft. The charismatic lineman quickly made an impact and was selected to the Pro Bowl in 1990 and in 1991. However, Brown died in a car accident during the summer of 1992. He was only 27 years old. After his death, the Eagles retired his No. 99 jersey. In tribute, Eagles' fans began using the slogan "Bring it home for Jerome," referencing a Super Bowl title. The slogan was still being used nearly 20 years after his death.

Eagles all-time leading receiver Harold Carmichael set an NFL record when he caught a pass in his 106th consecutive game in 1979. The 6-foot-8 wide receiver increased the record, which has since been broken, to 127 games. It was stopped when he suffered a back injury in the final game of the 1980 season against the Dallas Cowboys.

GLOSSARY

All-Pro

An award given to the top players at their position regardless of their conference. It is a high honor as there are fewer spots on the All-Pro team than on the Pro Bowl teams.

berth

A place, spot, or position, such as in the NFL playoffs.

comeback

Coming from behind to win a particular game.

dominant

The player or team that proves to be consistently better than the opponent.

draft

A system used by professional sports leagues to select new players in order to spread incoming talent among all teams.

enshrine

To be placed into, such as the Pro Football Hall of Fame.

franchise

An entire sports organization, including the players, coaches, and staff.

National Football Conference

One of two conferences to make up the NFL. As of 2010, there were 16 teams in the NFC.

postseason

Games played in the playoffs by the top teams after the regular season schedule has been completed.

Pro Bowl

A game after the regular season in which the top players from the American Football Conference (AFC) play against the top players from the National Football Conference (NFC).

rookie

A first-year professional athlete.

FOR MORE INFORMATION

Further Reading

Didinger, Ray. *The Eagles Encyclopedia.* Philadelphia, PA: Temple University Press, 2005.

Gordon, Robert. *Game of My Life Philadelphia Eagles: Memorable Stories of Eagles Football.* Champaign, IL: Sports Publishing LLC, 2007.

Sports Illustrated. *The Football Book Expanded Edition.* New York: Sports Illustrated Books, 2009.

Web Links

To learn more about the Philadelphia Eagles, visit ABDO Publishing Company online at **www.abdopublishing.com**. Web sites about the Eagles are featured on our Book Links page. These links are routinely monitored and updated to provide the most current information available.

Places to Visit

Lehigh University
27 Memorial Drive West
Bethlehem, PA 18015
610-758-6868
www.philadelphiaeagles.com/news/trainingcamp.html
Lehigh is the home of Eagles training camp in the summer.

Lincoln Financial Field
Pattison Avenue at South 11th Street
Philadelphia, PA 19148
215-339-6700
www.lincolnfinancialfield.com
The stadium has been the venue for Eagles home games since 2003.

Pro Football Hall of Fame
2121 George Halas Drive Northwest
Canton, OH 44708
330-456-8207
www.profootballhof.com
This hall of fame and museum highlights the greatest players and moments in the history of the NFL. Seventeen people affiliated with the Eagles are enshrined, including two-way stars Pete Pihos and Chuck Bednarik and defensive end Reggie White.

INDEX

About the Author

Tom Robinson is a sportswriter and an author and editor of educational books. The Clarks Summit, Pennsylvania, resident has covered National Football League games and issues during three decades of writing about sports. He has written more than 20 books for young readers.